THE JOURNEY TO SIMPLE PASSIVE CASHFLOW

THE JOURNEY TO SIMPLE PASSIVE CASHFLOW

REAL ESTATE INVESTING FOR THE WORKING PROFESSIONAL

LANE KAWAOKA

JONES MEDIA
PUBLISHING

Printed in the United States of America

ISBN: 978-1-948382-24-3 paperback
JMP2021.3

CONTENTS

INTRODUCTION

Back in 2009, I purchased my first rental property. I did so without any experience or knowledge about how to be a landlord, including where or even what to buy. No one in my family or friend circle had owned rental real estate. I did not know how to even run the numbers (we will give you the rental property analyser later in this book). *Sounds crazy, right?*

And so I became an accidental landlord. I didn't consciously go into buying this first property. I followed the old financial dogma: "Go to school, study hard, and get a good job." I became an engineer and, following the advice of my parents, saved up my money to buy my first house in Seattle, Washington (a *primary market* that we'll discuss later in this book). I've since learned *not* to buy properties in primary markets like Hawaii, California, Washington, New York, Miami, to name a few . . . but I simply didn't know any better at the time because I listened to all the unsophisticated mom-and-pop investor advice out there.

As a young professional, just a few years out of college, I was mostly out working on the road; the new guy *always* gets sent out. So, there I was: I had purchased a home that I was barely around to enjoy!

The house cost me $357,000, and I had to come up with a 20 percent down payment. So, I had to save about $80,000. I did just that in my first couple years of working as an engineer. But, because I was never home, I decided to call one of my old landlords from college. At the time, I didn't realize this person was a property manager and I asked, "Hey, can you rent out my property?"

After that call, she came over and we signed some paperwork. About a week later, she had found someone who wanted to rent my house for $2,200 a month. And—just like that—I moved out all my stuff and decided to live on the road and off of company expenses for the next few years. I think I was able to save $60,000 to $100,000 per year by doing this, which—spoiler alert—went to saving up for more down payments on future rental properties.

My mortgage interest taxes and insurance for that first property totaled around $1,600 a month. So, picture a young twentysomething year old with a cool $600 extra a month. Talk about easy money! That was a lot of beer money for me back then! More importantly, this was also when I got the taste of cashflow.

At the time, I flew down to Las Vegas frequently because my company figured it was cheaper to fly me to Las Vegas for the weekends instead of all the way to my home location in Seattle. I suddenly had $600 worth of extra spending money per month that I was able to spend freely. It was pretty much like playing with "house money." And that mindset lasted for a few months.

Once the novelty wore off, I started to broaden my thinking; I was frustrated at work (I worked as a construction supervisor managing between forty and fifty union-based construction workers who were my parents age), and I realized getting more rentals and passive cashflow could be the way out of working over twelve-hour days and living in motel rooms out in the wild blue yonder.

I started to really think about the numbers and how much money I was making once my property manager got a tenant in place. It's a no brainer! At first you're only thinking about the *cashflow*, right? The amount of money that the rental is kicking off every month; of course, some months you might make more and some you might make less, but overall you're making a pretty good return. What most people don't realize with rental real estate is that you're making money four ways—mortgage paydown, tax benefits, appreciation, and the aforementioned cashflow.

I realized I was able to make maybe about 30 percent a year on my initial investment. Then, I scratched my head . . . *Why the heck do I keep putting money into my 401(k) and maxing that thing out? Why am I supposedly making only 8–10 percent there? Where is my money going if I can do two to three times that with a simple rental property? Where is everyone else's money going?* Who stole it?

It didn't seem like a great deal. In fact, I had felt lied too! You know that feeling when you find that same pair of Nike's you bought at Neiman Marcus or Nordstrom was more expensive than Macy's or elsewhere on the interwebs . . . Who am I kidding? Most of you folks don't shop at Neiman

Marcus . . . you don't read a book on finances or investing if you're a "retail" shopper. But why are there so many "retail" investors?

This is when I started to learn the difference between those who invest on Wall Street and others who choose to take their financial future into their own hands, investing in real assets like properties and growing their money at multiples greater than the average person who remains at their day jobs until their 70s or 80s.

Yup, you guessed it! As an engineer, I started to build a spreadsheet, projecting the years and decades down the line. I would be able to retire much, much earlier than my parents thought they could, and then I started to become obsessed with this *Journey to Simple Passive Cashflow*.

While there are so many real-estate-guru programs out there, they mostly just fill your head with tons of mindset and motivation but zero tactical steps to take effective *action*. Most of these guru programs sell to broke guys trying to get rich quick, by selling hope and dreams. When I was starting out, there was nothing for the high-paid working (busy) professional like me.

THIS BOOK IS FOR THE PERSON WHO IS STUCK AT THEIR HIGH PAYING JOB WHO WANTS TO PRUDENTLY BUILD THEIR WEALTH THE WAY THE WEALTHY QUIETLY DO.

You haven't quite put your finger on it, but there's something more to life than going to work and getting a paycheck. Unfortunately, you're in a system that has been rigged against you with 401(k)s, mutual funds, and other retail investments.

One of the saddest things I see hardworking people do is buying a house to live in (not a rental) at the start of their financial journeys. I think this is one of the *worst* financial mistakes you can make. While writing this book, I have bought two houses to live in but now choose to rent because it is much more advantageous to do so. After working with my clients to achieve the goal of getting their net worth from $1 million to $10 million, I now believe that one should not buy a house unless their net worth is two to three times the price of their primary residence.

Financial independence is not for everybody, but it is for the worthy. Welcome to the *Journey to Simple Passive Cashflow*.

I've since built a $750 million dollar real estate portfolio that all started with that single-family home in 2009 . . . and now I want to share everything I learned along the way, with you.

CHAPTER 1

MY STORY

My background is very similar to many of you who are reading this. I call it the "linear path," where we're all told to be frugal with our money, not go into debt, study hard in school, work hard at our jobs, save to buy a home, have 2.1 kids, and *then* we will be able to enjoy retirement when we're sixty-two to eighty years old . . . after years *and years* of being frugal and working within the system.

I was introduced to simple passive cashflow in the form of rental income very early. It accidentally opened the world up for me, and it took me about a decade to achieve *Accredited investor* status. I started to uncover a world of how average people were creating generational wealth for themselves and their future families by investing in passive real estate investments—with a few methods available to those like yourself with a good paying job and current finances in shape (most folks out there are broke and come to real estate because they hear it framed as a get rich-quick-scheme).

The truth is, it's all pretty simple, but it's just underneath a lot of financial dogma that keeps a lot of hard working folks like yourself trapped in the system.

Back in grade school, I just happened to be good at math and science, so I unconsciously walked down this path of earning an engineering degree (then a master's degree), getting my professional engineering license (PE), and working for a Fortune 50 company. Sure, I earned a higher salary that allowed me a certain lifestyle. But I soon realized a few things . . .

My work wasn't very fun. I got stuck out in the field, supervising men in their fifties and sixties, and other union-based workers. I was out there in the cold and the rain on construction projects to supervise these guys. I think a lot of people find that when you get paid a lot, it is very stressful. I was traveling all the time for work. Sure, with 100 percent travel came hundreds of thousands of frequent flyer points and first class all the time, but I saw the other people around me, people such as the corporate slaves up in first class who probably had a family that never saw them or a family that had left them, and that's not what I wanted.

After a few years into my young career, I knew I wasn't that great of an engineer. After all, I had a 3.1 GPA in college—heck, I knew it back then. I wasn't the employee who would be thrusted up the corporate ladder who was "red circled" for higher level positions. I saw my path ahead, to work at this job for forty or fifty more years, eventually paying off my house. I thought I was being smarter than my peers by being frugal and essentially maxing out my 401(k) and Roth accounts every year while investing in index funds and following the Boglehead and FIRE blogs.

And then I bought my first rental property. And I saw myself making two to three times more with my money in that *one* rental property than what my money was getting in the "retail" financial product world of stocks/bonds, mutual funds, and index funds.

My parents paid down their house diligently through decades of white-knuckling. Most people like them will probably retire with about $1 million in assets, most of it locked up in their home equity. Or house rich, cash poor. You might go on a few vacations with your two to four weeks of vacation throughout the years. But when you get into your golden years, you're probably going to get to a point where you can't physically enjoy your meager wealth, and it'll all be too late.

The systematic approach we advocate for—instead of the traditional method of financial wealth building—is based on cashflow. By only buying assets such as rental real estate, which more than pays for all its expenses every month, is a very prudent and safe way of building wealth. What we're doing here is we're creating streams of income *today*. And it's a diversified pool of income. Most people have this idea of accumulation-theory, but in the case of my parents and thousands or millions of other baby boomers out there, even for the most frugal of white-knucklers, I don't see their net worth surpassing much more than $1–$1.5 million in their lifetime. Most of my clients, living the simple-passive-cashflow lifestyle, are able to well surpass the $4.5 million threshold and in a fraction of the time.

There's a better way. And there's a safer way. There's a way for you and most of my clients to gain financial freedom in less than ten years. Money's not everything, but it affords you the freedom to do what you want, with whom you want, where you want, and when you want.

It gives you options. Most people never ask themselves, *What is my highest and best use other than working at my day job?* After I have enough money that I don't need to trade my time for money, what else can I do? What legacy can I leave behind?

Most people, quite frankly, don't have very much. One-million dollars is not much of a platform to do much of anything—that amount is just putting on your own oxygen mask for meager survival. There are a lot of people with doctorate degrees, master's degrees, and very useful undergraduate degrees who are stuck working, trading time for money. How did I break the cycle?

After that first purchase in 2009, I decided to buy another duplex in Seattle in 2012. At this time, I started to learn that you shouldn't go to the high-end luxury, A-class properties or the warzone, F- and D-class properties, which are ridden with headaches and poor collections. It's actually preferable to be in the middle, like the B- and C-class properties. So, instead of an A-class property (like my first property in an ideal submarket in North Seattle), my second purchase was more of a B plus (white/blue collar tenant in West Seattle).

Around 2012, prices were going up and I started to realize that I wasn't getting as much rental income per my rental property acquisition price. I was getting a little desperate because the numbers weren't working as well as a couple years prior. So I started to look around for other options, one of which was to buy properties from an auction.

Buying properties from auction is another tactic in the bag of tricks of the no-money, broke folks who are trying to get rich quick. These properties are typically more distressed properties. And it's *not* worth the risk for higher net worth and higher-paid busy professionals like you. I remember going to one of these real estate clubs, where every Thursday they would hold a meeting prior to the auction to discuss the properties up for grabs. It was like a war room/fantasy football meeting, just a little more professional. I'd look around the room, where they served a crappy spaghetti dinner, and I realized it was just a bunch of old, unsophisticated investors from Microsoft who just had *too* much money (hashtag dumb-money, as the kids would call it).

I quickly realized these other guys didn't know anything; they only *thought* they were getting a good deal. And, sure, they would probably be okay because real estate typically appreciates in value, but at that point I made the choice to be more of a cashflow investor. Most people have the idea that they need to invest for accumulation; they're trying to build a large amount of money, say $2–4 million, to live off of in retirement. I believe that line of thinking is *flawed*.

Once you get up to that retirement point—when you're *older*—you'll want to be able to live off of the streams of cashflow. So, I say, Why not begin with the end in mind and start to build these mini cashflow streams today? Let's just call them *mini pensions* instead of banking on your pension from your company or social security (we all know how unreliable companies and state/city governments are these days). The nice thing about the cashflow/mini pension/simple passive cashflow method is you can eat off of the cashflow stream today.

But if you're like me, you're not going to use this cashflow stream to buy a new car, home, or pool, but maybe your kids' private school education or college. Especially if you have a good paying day job that more than pays today's bills and puts food on your table, you're likely to use these streams of income to buy more and more properties, generating more streams of income. This is essentially what I did with my extra $600 a month from that very first property. Now, I had an additional $1,000 per month to go purchase another property more quickly. In those first three to four years, I was moving like a turtle, saving my money. Granted, I was still living on the road at this time as a single, super frugal guy.

I was saving upwards of $80,000 to $100,000 a year. Sometimes I'd even make a game out of it, only spending $100 or less a week to maximize my savings. I'd drive back home from a work trip and eat at buffet on the company's dime. Then, I wouldn't eat the next day (intermittent fast). While I'm not advocating for this lifestyle per se, this is how I buckled down and saved money.** Note: most of my younger clients are able to save at least $10,000, whereas those over the age of forty are able to save $30,000–50,000+ a year.

Around 2012, the market reached an inflection point where I wasn't able to cashflow in a primary (tier 1) market like Seattle. Other notable primary (tier 1) markets that we stay away from because

---

* A bit of humor here, but check out http://simplepassivecashflow.com/cheapo/ for a list of things I did to save money. Some of which I am not entirely proud of.

they are more cyclical in nature are California, Hawaii, New York and Miami, to name a few.

This is when I started seeking out remote *turnkey rentals* (a fully renovated home or 2–4 units that an investor can purchase and immediately rent out) that were in a secondary or tertiary market, where the numbers made more sense. I bought one such property in Birmingham, Alabama, for about $70,000. The monthly rent was $850. So, I was beating the 1 percent rent-to-value ratio that is *so* critical for cashflow. It was a B property and it worked! The crazy thing was that I never saw it and never even interacted with it. I had a property manager doing everything. I built a team of people, and I got lucky because the wrong people will definitely screw you over. I found some loose referrals, and that was how I started to systemize investing remotely. Eventually, I jumped off the cyclical appreciation bandwagon and got on the steady cashflow game. I sold off the two Seattle properties and went into eleven rentals in 2015 (Birmingham, Atlanta, Indianapolis, Pennsylvania).

When I purchased my first rental, I discovered I could make 20–30 percent returns on my investment; while running my 401(k) and stock portfolio, I was lucky enough to get a long-term gain of 8–10 percent.*

This was the epiphany I had when I first started investing: you don't have to be a complete expert at it and you don't have to waste so much time flipping houses, wholesaling houses, or playing the role of active investor.

WHY IS REAL ESTATE INVESTING BETTER?

Well, you get way more returns and you pay less taxes because of the tax benefits. And it's a hard asset that preserves its value.

The problem with the 401(k) plan is that you're trapped within the current set of offerings. One of those is the 401(k), 403(b), TSP, or 529 plan which grow tax-free . . . but what most people don't think or talk about is that you're going to have to pay the taxes *eventually*. There are four big reasons why I don't advocate for those under $1.5 million net worth to use any retirement accounts, including 401(k)s or Roth IRAs:

---

* For more information and breakdown of investment returns on a simple rental property, go to http://simplepassivecashflow.com/Returns/

1. These plans are all based on the idea that you're going to want to pay less taxes in the future when you start withdrawing from a retirement plan, which I think is completely opposite. This idea is predicated on you growing old, losing your large active/,ordinary/,W-2 income, and being in a *lower* tax bracket because your income is *less*. However, I'm more optimistic, and in fact, I know that in the future I'm going to make a lot *more* money when I get older; therefore, I will be in a *higher* tax bracket. So I want to pay my taxes today and get it out of a retirement account.

2. Let's look at where this country is going. We just pumped in trillions of dollars of stimulus recently, and this trend will continue. As long as America owns the world currency and has the best military, we'll continue to print money. How will we pay for all this? Most people will agree that taxes are going to go up, therefore, you want to pay taxes on your money now when you assume the rates will be lower than in the future. You have a choice to either pay your taxes today or in the future. If you agree with me, then you want to pay your taxes today. That's why I wouldn't want my money in one of these retirement accounts. *Qualified retirement plans* are the governments greatest

potential source of revenue: by having your money as any sort of qualified-retirement-plan money, you basically give the government the right to or lien to take whatever they want in the future. Still, you might say, "Well, maybe I'll do the Roth IRA, right? Because I can pay my taxes today rather than the future." Well, that brings me to my next point . . .

I want my money outside of these qualified retirement plans. Consider a self-directed IRA, IRA, 401(k), 403(b), and TSP: these are accounts where you're making money in this vehicle but you can't actually use the passive losses (deductions) that an investment produces. And this is what separates a mom-and-pop, single-family home landlord from a passive limited partner syndication investor. *Real estate syndication* (or property syndication) is a partnership between several investors. They combine their skills, resources, and capital to purchase and manage a property they otherwise couldn't afford.

3. Wealthy investors have a higher level of sophistication on taxes. They know they are able to use the passive losses and bonus depreciation from these larger deals to offset ordinary income. Plus, if they implement a real

estate professional status on their taxes, they can lower their overall tax rate by shielding their high W-2 income from their day job.

If this is new to you, don't worry: I didn't know this stuff when I started investing, and quite frankly, most people—even CPAs—are totally oblivious to the power of real estate losses. Basically a real estate investment will likely produce you a positive gain from cashflow, but the trick is being able to take the paper losses that come from depreciating the asset. In single-family homes, you're able to deduct one twenty-seventh over twenty-seven years of the buildings value. You can't deduct the land value because dirt doesn't depreciate; but the property value can be deducted twenty-seventh of the value for twenty-seven years. So, in theory, you could have an investment that has a negative paper loss associated with it. You're making money cashflow-wise, getting the appreciation, and your mortgage is paid down all the while that depreciation could take you into the red—and that's a good thing, because you normally pay taxes on the gains, but if you're able to drive your gains down, you then pay little to no taxes; check out screenshots of my tax return at http://simplepassivecashflow.com/tax/! Going back to why to avoid retirement plans:

you don't get any of these precious passive losses if you're investing via a retirement account.

4. The fourth and final reason why I don't like these qualified retirement plans is because you can only start to pull out the money when you're old or else you get penalized. I retired well before I was forty years old. And I think a lot of people reading this book can retire in five to ten years! This is well before the government allows you to touch your retirement funds.

When I had bunch of properties in 2015, I initially had this idea that I'd have them all paid off. Why? Well, that's what you hear when you hang out with the wrong people. But sophisticated investors don't completely pay off their properties; in fact, they use debt like a tool to acquire more and more properties, thereby increasing their cashflow. And as far as asset protection goes, having paid off properties is one of the dumbest things you can do because now everybody knows where your money is at, making you a big target for a lawsuit. Encumbering your properties with debt is one of the most basic forms of asset protection.

From a net worth and cashflow perspective, utilizing prudent debt is the *smart* thing to do. One big mistake that investors make is that they don't leverage their assets. Let's say the market price of the property goes up, therefore, their equity position goes up because there's a tenant paying down their mortgage . . . unfortunately, their *return on equity* goes *down* over the years. Maybe you're making 30 percent or more a year. But as your property appreciates, you have more equity in the property, and that return of equity goes down.*

Sophisticated investors pay attention to the return of equity; people say, "Buy and never sell," but that's not always true. You can buy and then you might sell the asset or trade it to keep that return on equity high. What we like to do is refinance our lazy equity out and remain in a cashflowing deal with none of our original capital in there . . . we call this infinite returns. Let's use a property that you've paid 100 percent off—you own the property outright—as a classic example. You're probably making less than what you could be making with a US savings bond or sub 3 percent a year. Also it's really dumb, in my opinion, to take on that much litigation liability.

---

* For more information and a downloadable spreadsheet to start to analyze where your lazy equity is hiding, go to http://simplepassivecashflow.com/ROE/

It's not worth it . . . but there *is* a sweet spot with a good amount to leverage to optimize the returns and cashflow. There's a point at which you can always sell or refinance and get that leverage point higher. Personally, when I'm making less than 15–20 percent a year, I'm looking to do a refinance or another capital event like selling.

When you have ten or twenty, even thirty rentals, refinancing or selling, then buying again can become quite the chore. And you're going to make your lending broker rich if you follow their loaded advice of getting an all-in-one portfolio loan. I started to feel the growing pains of a larger portfolio around 2015, when I had eleven rentals. About this time is when I started to pay my way into masterminds and other high-level groups. When you go to the local real estate investment association, or REIA, or find free online forums, what you're really doing is interacting with newbies and broke guys—these are guys who don't have good jobs and guys who don't have any money. Their net worth is most likely less than $250,000 and most aren't even investing. It's a complete waste of time, especially for a working busy professional like yourself. Most of the local in-person meetings have the group think mentality of investing where they live which, if you're an investor—especially one who lives in a primary market like California, Washington, Hawaii, New York, Boston, Washington, DC— you're not going to be able to find cashflow in your local area. Going to these local groups or free online forums isn't going to help you—but it might make you want to take a shower after.

In 2015, I had eleven rentals, which is a pretty good sample size to describe what the heck actually happens in that situation. Of course, I had all professional, third-party property management teams. I don't advocate anybody to manage these properties by themselves. That's what your grandma and grandpa did back in the day. And that's why they only had one or two rental properties and why it took them so long to get to financial freedom. Always, *always* get a third-party property manager. Focus on being an investor, *not a landlord.*

With my eleven rental properties, I had an eviction or two each year, which wasn't too much of an issue. I also had some kind of major catastrophe happen perhaps three or four times a year. Maybe a tree falls on the house or there's a flooded basement due to a rainstorm or a toilet/ plumbing issue. These things happen. As an investor, you're managing the manager who's working to remedy these situations. And you're just approving and ensuring they're being a good steward with your asset. With eleven rentals, at about a few thousand dollars of passive household a month, you're doing alright.[*]

Most of my investors shoot for a goal of having $10,000 passive income a month. In theory, you'd need to take my eleven rentals and multiply them by three. Now, you're multiplying that exception frequency and talking about an eviction every other month, and some kind of big catastrophe that happens every few weeks. And then you start to realize these types of investments are *unscalable*. That's not even taking into account the fact that it's *very* hard to really leverage these assets.

With these eleven rental properties, one out of three properties lost money in a year. Think about it. Say a HVAC goes out or there is another large repair: it might put the property in the red for the entire year. Overall, however, I was making about $3,000 of passive cashflow a month from the portfolio as a whole. I had already come a long way from where I'd started back in 2009, but I needed more to hit my goals— quit my day job— and to find an easier way to scale.

---

[*] Get our free rental property analyser to have a better understanding of padding your expenses go to http://simplepassivecashflow.com/Analyser/

This is why I started to pay to get into higher level masterminds. And this is where I found my people—other highly paid doctors, lawyers, engineers, and high-paid working professionals—people who were at my level and beyond to get the real strategy that went beyond, the stale books and regurgitated advice in podcast-land.

It was common among this circle to find other investors who owned respectable-sized rental property portfolios, but they were like, the hell with that! Their attitude resonated with me; this is where this new world opened up. Buying my own rentals, getting my net worth to $600k, and investing in rental properties was the prerequisite to build relationships with these people. Soon I discovered syndication deals that did cost segregations and extracted plenty of passive losses, multitudes more than my single-family rentals per dollar invested. This I found was the first step to unlocking all these other wealth-building strategies, like paying less taxes, utilizing real estate professional status to offset ordinary income, and so on. And then infinite banking using whole life, overfunded insurance and other more legacy creation activities.

I realized a lot of this stuff was very simple, but it was *very* different than what my parents had taught me or what others may teach you through classes, groups, and forums—certainly not what your friends and coworkers talk about.

I made a point to interact with the *right* people, and I picked up different tactics and strategies by way of osmosis. I leveled up and started to get traction! From 2009 to 2015, I went from zero to eleven rentals. As of 2021, I own over 5,000 rental units.

There is a saying, "Money talks but wealth whispers." A lot of gurus teach broke guys about getting rich by flipping homes or doing these rehab strategies. But the wealthy quietly go into boring cashflowing rentals, utilize changing best practices in tax/legal, and ultimately build legacies.

CHAPTER 2

WHY CASHFLOWING REAL ESTATE?

You have the ability to make money four ways with real estate: (1) you have equity build up with the mortgage paid down with the heart, sweat, and tears of your tenants paying rent; (2) tax benefits; (3) appreciation of the property; and (4) cashflow is achieved by picking properties with the right rent-to-value ratio where your income exceeds your expenses on a monthly basis. And when you add these all up, you'll find that you're beating what you would be getting in the stock market by three or four times.

You're getting that equity built up minus your debt service because the majority of that goes to your debt service in the beginning, but a portion of that goes to equity buildup. So, with my first property, my *PITI mortgage* (principal, interest, taxes, and insurance—the sum components of a mortgage payment) was $1,600 a month. In the beginning, the majority of the loan is going to interest, but a few hundred bucks is going to pay down your principal balance and then at the end you cash that. You have to include this in the whole equation too.

The tax benefits can get a little complicated, but essentially you're able to write off the asset and—even though you're making cashflow—you can drive that negative and possibly lower your adjusted gross income (AGI), depending on where your AGI is and where you fall on the tax brackets.

The nice thing about real estate is it typically goes up. Normally a property will appreciate 2–3 percent just with the pace of inflation. And for every 2 percent it goes up, you're making 8–10 percent on your money because you're leveraged. However, we don't *count* on it going up because to us, appreciation is icing on top of the cake after the cashflow, mortgage paydown, and tax benefits.

When I had my first rental property, I took the "red pill" of money (*The Matrix* reference) and realized how fee structures work in retail financial products and how it hurts the average investor. Wall Street compensation is very heavy for those guys at the top. How else do they pay for these fancy banks at almost every street corner? And you hear these high executive salaries; they're just pushing paper. They're not creating value. I saw the dissonance between investing in something simple, like a single-family home where I made 20–30-percent-plus a year, versus my 401(k), where it was a roller coaster to make 8–10 percent per year.

I started to look more closely, reading the right materials and following the right people. We were all conditioned to pay no attention to the man behind that curtain. It's important to remember that the foot soldiers of Wall Street, where you put money blindly into the system, are financial planners who are commission-based and heavy-fee mutual fund portfolio managers. When you lose money, they still make their commission/fees. I think a lot of younger people are starting to realize that financial planners are just fancy suits and "nice" guys who don't know how to generate *real wealth.*

THE BIGGEST THING I LEARNED WHEN I STARTED TO HANG AROUND HIGH NET WORTH ACCREDITED INVESTORS IS THE GOLDEN RULE: *NEVER TAKE FINANCIAL ADVICE FROM PEOPLE WHO ARE NOT FINANCIALLY FREE.*

Financial planners are not financially free. They're out there hunting for commissions, and they're making money off your back and your hard work. These are not people from whom you should be taking financial advice.

I'd never had any money. I was taught the traditional way: put your money *into* the system. And the system works, unfortunately, right? Our parents will retire with a mere million dollars because they "white-knuckled it," which is the term for most frugal people who like to pay down their debt and have all of their money in their home.

And if they're "good citizens," they'll be able to retire with maybe seven figures in their bank account. And most will likely die without enjoying most of it. There are so many hardworking people out there who did everything they were supposed to: go to school, study hard, get a good job, work at a job, and so on. Now, you have to take care of your aging parents and your young kids. And you're just stuck in this constant rat race. And part of the reason it's this way is because the institutions are just taking a huge chunk. I mean, some people even estimate that a third of your earnings go straight up to hidden fees.

I bought properties that were 1 percent rent-to-value ratio and that were prudently cashflowing in most months. And I bought multiples of these. I diversified over different markets, and it wasn't like I got lucky or anything like that. I put emphasis on cashflow over gambling on appreciation. I wasn't doing a huge amount of work, flipping houses, taking a lot of risk. I just did the slow and steady way. By creating my own portfolio of rental properties, I was able to get off the "retail" path of investing in paper assets and was able to quit my day job within a decade of doing this.

Of course, I made a lot of mistakes along the way, which I will now share so that you can expedite your journey to simple passive cashflow!

CHAPTER 3

BECOMING AN ACCREDITED INVESTOR

Around 2012 the real estate market had bounced off the bottom of the 2008 recession, and prices were going up. I already had three rental units to my name that I had acquired with traditional 20 percent down payment financing. The first property I bought was entirely the wrong property that no one should buy, especially their first time around. It was in a primary market (Seattle), where the numbers did not work.

Today, I focus more on workforce housing, class B and C properties, because, in tough times or recessions, tenants tend to move out of A-class stuff and backfill into more *value-based* rentals. But, of course, I didn't know anything back then.

The second property I bought was a duplex in more of an A-minus/B-plus area. My rent-to-value ratio improved slightly from the first one, but it was still nowhere near the golden 1 percent rule: *the rent-to-value ratio is the monthly rent divided by the purchase price.*

I went to various local real estate clubs, but I kept finding wholesalers and flippers—a bunch of guys who just didn't have money. They weren't the pedigree of a working professional. They didn't make more than $60,000 a year. One event I went to early on was a war-room type of auction, where they would get investors together and talk about deals that came up via auction—which is a very risky way of investing and gets a lot of newbie investors intrigued, perhaps because of the allure of buying properties on the courthouse steps for supposedly pennies on the dollar. And they would give out some lame free spaghetti dinner to attract the cheap, easy, free-looking crowd to come in and create the atmosphere of investor frenzy. I tell a lot of investors (even high net worth investors) to spend at least 1–3 months learning about all investing techniques (flipping, wholesaling, tax-liens) to understand that most of these strategies are for those with little money or abundance of time. In the end, the most boring cashflowing investments are what the wealthy do.

My immediate goal at the time was to quit my day job, which required cashflow from rentals to replace my income.

This is where I started my search to go out of state, because, at the time, I was hearing of these mythical creatures called *turnkey rentals*. There is no standard for a turnkey rental, but it is essentially a property where a rehabber acquires a dilapidated property and resurrects it from the dead by fixing up all the major components: the roof, the electrical, the plumbing, new paint, fresh countertops, sometimes even putting a tenant in there too and then sells it to passive investors like us who are looking for a finished turnkey product to put into our portfolio.

I realized Seattle wasn't a good market to be investing for cashflow in 2012. I started looking into other cities I'd never visited in order to buy sights unseen. I started my search and eventually found a place in Birmingham, Alabama.

I worked with a turnkey rental provider and became engaged with a property management company that was a third party to the person who was selling me the property. I also got a hold of a lending broker who worked with a lot of out-of-state, non-owner occupied property folks. One of the biggest mistakes I see investors making is they work with the lending broker who got them their primary residence, which is completely different than buying an out-of-state rental property. Oftentimes, when you go to one of these larger banks, you're working with an incompetent loan officer. I did a bit of networking around with other pure passive investors who were also doing this. I also received recommendations from the brokers I was working with. I made sure to take everything with a grain of salt, and I put more emphasis on working with those who didn't have any skin in the game or going to be paid some sort of referral fee.

I found more success working with these folks rather than those whom you can talk to on free internet forums, where the users are broke guys just looking to *get rich quick*. The way we're doing things—via cashflow—is *not* a get rich quick scheme but rather a get rich *surely* situation. So, I found a good property manager, knowing he could vet properties that I wouldn't see in person, because, yes, I was buying these properties sight unseen.

However, I was assembling a team to assist me with due diligence. I hired a property inspector who walked the property to make sure I didn't buy a lemon. When I was working with a lender, they were also doing their due diligence in the title work and getting the appraisal. The property manager helped me bring everything together and made sure this was a good rental with the rents that I anticipated. Putting my first out-of-state rental into operation went pretty smoothly out of the gate, and I was like, *Wow, I get a lot more rent, a lot more revenue per the dollar than compared to the Seattle properties I owned at the time.* I realized I needed to get rid of my properties in Seattle and go all-in on this cashflow based investing! You can read more about this process here: http://simplepassivecashflow.com/turnkey/

Back in 2010 when I was just a newbie landlord, I did not know what to expect in terms of my monthly profit and losses. As you move along into rental ownership, you learn things are going to break and there might be some other expenses. Later, I discovered that most months I made money and sometimes I lost money—that expenses, vacancies, and evictions were just part of the game.

I developed an analyser that breaks down all the expenses you may incur and will likely incur, and those you should probably calculate and assume you're going to incur. Say you have a rental property that rents for $1,000 per month, 10 percent is usually going to repairs and maintenance. There's going to be plumbing and other small repairs here and there. Another 10 percent will go to your property manager.

Again, I always have investors get a third-party property manager. You hear most unsophisticated mom-and-pop landlord investors doing it themselves, but I believe this is the wrong way to do it. If you're reading this book and make a good professional salary, your highest and best use is at your day job or playing around with your kids and having a great life rather than screwing around with making repairs at an hourly rate of less than $50. So, we're paying our property manager and we're also paying them some lease-up fees, and we're going to have some vacancy there too. So, that takes us down another 10 percent. It's certainly not free to run a rental property.

We're also going to have some large capital-expenditure issues that come up every five to twenty years. For example, replacing the roof every ten to twenty years or so, maybe thirty if you're lucky. So money needs to go into some kind of slush account, whether you keep it in a bank account or you just commingle it with your personal funds. If you're a homeowner, you totally understand what I'm talking about. Large things break. Of course, you have to pay your mortgage, interest taxes, insurance, or PITI, so what's leftover is likely a very small portion of your income. And *that* is our cashflow.

One of the biggest mistakes I hear unsophisticated investors say is that their monthly rent is $1,000 and so their mortgage (PITI, or principal, interest, taxes, and insurance) is $500. And they say they're cashflowing at $500. That's *incorrect*. You need to include *all* of your expenses. And once you do that, you'll have your true cashflow number.* Feel free to download my rental property analyser at http://simplepassivecashflow.com/analyser/ to understand the numbers.

Today, my team and I go after 1 percent rent-to-value ratio properties, which kind of takes away a lot of the coastal markets, including the whole state of California, as well as Hawaii, Seattle, Portland, New York, Boston, and DC. We're actually targeting markets that are found more often in red states. Politics aside, as a landlord

---

* A lot of this information can be found in my e-course, or you can go to http://simple-passivecashflow.com/turnkey/ to learn more.

you want to be in areas where the landlord laws are on your side.

In some states, the landlord laws tip very much in favor of the tenant, and it can take forever to evict a tenant who isn't paying. I also like to invest in *emerging markets,* where the population is increasing. Due to economic growth, these are typically found in more red states and southern states as the population is moving from colder climates to warmer ones. I also try to stay in secondary and tertiary markets. So, these are large cities, with more than a quarter million population.

I found that I was making a lot more money doing this type of investing than I ever was in stocks and mutual funds around the same time. I also sold all those rental properties in Seattle, and I did a *1031 exchange* to nine out-of-state properties. This exchange is a swap of one investment property for another that allows capital gains taxes to be deferred.

By 2015 I had eleven rentals; these included five properties in Atlanta, four in Birmingham, one in Indianapolis, and one in Pennsylvania. Around this time, I started to realize that rental properties were *not* scalable. Whenever you own a rental property, as the property appreciates and the tenants pay down your mortgage for you, if any of your principal increases (which is a good thing), unfortunately, your return on equity goes down.

Sophisticated investors *always* pay attention to the return on equity. When you have so many rentals, it is impractical to get refinances on all your properties. You're going to make your lender very rich doing this. And you're also going to go crazy with all the friction costs and all the headaches (tenants, termites, toilets) even with good property managers. With eleven rentals, I had an eviction or two every year; I've probably had more than six evictions altogether. And about a third of the time, it resulted in a $5,000 to $20,000 repair bill. As these crappy tenants screwed up the property and left, I had no recourse to collect from them. Check out my YouTube Channel to see that infamous walkthrough of my trashed property that an evicted tenant left me.

The evictions were one thing, but just on a day-to-day or a month-to-month basis, you're going to have repairs and maintenance, which is fine because the property manager takes care of most of this. Most of these repairs aren't a huge issue moneywise. The cashflow more than overcomes this stuff, but your role is to manage the property manager, to make sure they take care of these repairs in a timely and cost-effective fashion.

If you want to get to where most of my clients' goals are, which is that magic $10,000 of passive cashflow a month, just imagine how your life would be totally different . . . but you're going to have to multiply all those rental properties and headaches by *three since my eleven rentals only gave me $3,000 of cashflow per month.* So, instead of an eviction or two every year, you're talking about an eviction every single quarter; and instead of a big catastrophe happening every quarter, you're talking about one every few weeks potentially.

I saw the writing on the wall and then I started to search for that next thing. I didn't know what it was, but I started to pay money to level up my network. I had grown past the free stuff on the internet and the local communities; I still didn't have a tribe though.

From 2009 to 2015, I did most of this all by my lonesome—and it was *slow*. My net worth grew from zero to just shy of a million dollars in six years. I took it to several thousand rental units in the coming years, very quickly.

I also contributed a hundred percent of my growth to joining different mastermind groups and getting around other high net worth Accredited investors (i.e., professionals who are looking to build their network with others to start on their journey to financial freedom). The funny thing was that many of these people were ex-landlords and small-time investors like how I started. They all joked after becoming Accredited investors that there wasn't a single good reason for owning direct rentals or small multifamily properties on their own. Many of them invested in private placements and syndications, where they are passive investors. They have no debt to their names and they have very little to no liability as an limited partner (LP) in a deal. And they're diversified over different partners, different geographic areas, different deals and asset classes, and different business plans—all this without having to really lift a finger, other than to sign some paperwork in the beginning and wire funds out.

One of the biggest blind spots investors have is building your network with other pure passive, high net worth investors. A lot of people just don't realize this. At first, I operated as an investor group of one (me, myself, and I). I didn't talk to anybody; as an engineer, I'm a bit of an introvert.

It wasn't necessarily in my nature to branch out, talk to others, and get help. And it's hard to find people on the same path as you, in your same pedigree, as a highly paid working professional!

It wasn't until 2013 that I started to see my first private placement and syndication deal. And, just like most people when they see that first deal, I was like, *Wow, this is really cool.* It made me feel really special—part of a secret club—little did I know that this first deal I went into was a sucker deal designed to scam newbies. Somebody referred me over to one particular operator, and my mistake was that I did not know the guy making the referral. I didn't know that the referral was bogus or he was potentially getting a kickback, but I invested about $45,000. And this was my first foray into passive investing. I essentially invested with the *wrong* person, who ran the deal into the ground.[*]

Looking back on it, there were several lessons learned:

First, this deal wasn't structured via a Regulation D 506(b) or 506(c) deal. There was very little recourse, and it wasn't filed with the United States Securities and Exchange Commission.

[*] http://simplepassivecashflow.com/fail/

Second, the person I found this contact from was an unverified source. Again, the gold standard—and how I find people to work with today—is having a network of people whom I trust and I call my friends. And they have a wide breadth of people that they know. Whenever I find somebody I haven't met before, I can go to my trusted network and see what the scoop is with this person.

I essentially lost all my money on this deal. I needed to build relationships with other passive investors so that I would have a sounding board to make sure I didn't invest with a shyster in the future.

I AM URGING YOU TO REALLY GET OUT OF YOUR CURRENT BOX.

When your net worth is under half a million dollars. You can go do it on your own. You're working with property managers, brokers, and so on, but when you become more of an Accredited investor, especially investing in private placements and syndications, and especially as you start to expand your wealth-building techniques to infinite banking, legal, and tax tactics, it's all going to come down to your network. As the saying goes, your network is your *net worth*. And it is critical for an Accredited investor to build a community of their own around them.

From 2009 to 2015 I stayed in my shell, investing on my own and went from zero to eleven rentals. From 2015 to 2021 I went to 6,000 rentals, and it wouldn't have been possible if I had stayed in my shell. When I started to join these mastermind groups, I had gone in with the intention of being an operator/GP. This was going to eventually replace my engineering career; I was going to do this full time. I must have spent over six figures to get individual coaching and attend mastermind groups. This helped me build the portfolio today of dozens of apartment buildings that we own and operate. What I noticed out there was what really helped me get to the next level—having a peer group of my own.

There are a lot of groups out there for people who want to be operators trying to run their own deals, but they're very expensive. A lot of these are going to cost you well over $25,000 a year. But what I realized as I talked to dozens and dozens of investors every single week is that there was a *big* need for passive investors who weren't necessarily going to be operators or general partners. They just wanted a good place to invest and have a peer group while still working in their six-figure-plus salary and managing their growing families. I sought to create something that, in as little as four to five hours a month, a passive investor could join a pre-selected community of other pure passive investors to call and source due diligence, swap best practices for tax and legal, and take these organic relationships into the future.

As I started to interact with family offices on my investment side, I realized there's a layer of individuals out there that are called "family office" folks. These are defined as $100 million families and above. The Rockefeller's are a great example of this.

But what do you do when your net worth is $1 million and you're trying to get to $10 million?

Well, I sought to create a network in a group-coaching format of developing family offices in the Family Office Ohana Mastermind, or FOOM for short. In this group, we have over seventy-five investors, most of whom are Accredited, and they're all trying to do the same thing while working a full-time day job and trying to build a legacy that won't just get blown by spoiled children/grandchildren.

I was frustrated by the numerous investing educational programs out there that gouged investors, charging them $20,000, $35,000, even $50,000 dollars annually. Many of these people that I feel bad for could not afford these expensive coaching options and should have used it as a down payment for the actual first investment.

So, a typical Family Office Ohana Mastermind client will come into our group. They'll typically be brand new to the world of alternative investing. They may or may not have owned a rental property in the past, but they are certainly an Accredited investor with at least $1 million dollars net worth, or they make over $250,000/ year at their day job. Most people come in wanting to find a peer network of other passive investors to figure out who to work with (and, more importantly, who to stay away from) in this sea of private placements. One third of the curriculum of a family office client is to source and analyze deals. But while investing in stronger yielding investments that are more securely backed by hard assets, they unlock *passive activity losses*, or PALS.

We like PALS. These passive activity losses allow us to offset passive income, which come off of our passive investments because we're about to depreciate the real estate's value over time. But it also has potential to offset our ordinary income, which we derive from our W-2 salaries or business income. One way we can do this is to implement "real estate professional" strategy on our taxes. We work with clients to develop a strategy based on their family-organization structure. A typical client might be a highly paid doctor with a stay-at-home spouse. And the stay-at-home spouse is a great candidate to achieve that real estate professional status. Now, this income earner can drive their ordinary income down via their passive losses to make their AGI lower. It's a beautiful thing when a spouse can stay at home to raise a family, while the family pays less in taxes and ultimately brings in more net income. This is a prime example of how the wealthy are playing a different game.

Everybody is concerned about the future president's tax brackets and how they hurt the higher income earners. Personally, I don't make too much active income, therefore, I'm not taxed. And a lot of passive investors in dozens of syndication deals are swimming in hundreds of thousands of dollars of passive activity losses.

And they don't have to pay taxes if they don't want to. This is another reason why you do not want to be a house flipper or private money lender, because that income is ordinary, not passive income, and there are no PALS.

Paying zero taxes probably sounds crazy to most folks . . . but a lot of people are getting these passive activity losses because they are investing in the economy. And in our country, the tax code is written to incentivize certain behaviors—such as investors, like us, putting money into things this country needs (like workforce housing and apartments, mobile home parks, self-storage units, office spaces, etc.). As an investor, you need to realize that taxes are your number one expense in life. And you need to empower yourself; this is why we educate and train our FOOM members to invest, or to at least understand tax codes to be able to have intelligent conversations and steer the ship with their CPA.

In most cases clients change their CPA because most CPAs are just unaware of these tactics. But even if you have an informed CPA, unless you as the client have a basic understanding of taxes, I would not expect your CPA to implement optimal tax plans for you.

It makes sense why they're not: why deviate from what's normal and make their lives more difficult? When I was an employee, I'll be honest: I always did everything the easiest way, right? I mean, that's exactly why these CPAs do it this way; they haven't figured out how to use the tax code how the wealthy do. We collectively educate and pull best practices so that we can steer the ship with our tax and legal professionals, getting the best bang for our dollar. My goal is to empower investors with this stuff so that they can steer the ship with their team of professionals (which we always refer to), but we need to empower ourselves to be the architects of our Family Office.

A typical client will come into our group, understand how to invest in syndications, do basic due diligence on deals, and develop a network with other pure passive investors to find future sustainable deal flows to invest in. They will also learn how to use the tax benefits on their taxes to be able to keep more money at the end of the day, creating a harmonious cycle called the *simple passive cashflow gravy train*. They can use the extra money in more investments to get even more tax benefits. And they can also fund infinite banking policies, creating a legacy wealth tax-free and litigation-free. High net worth

Accredited investors do things very differently than what most of us learned from our parents and peers.

Of course, this stuff changes every couple of years as congress or presidency changes and different political agendas change. But we always find ourselves in a heads-I-win-tails-I-win situation. Knowledge is power when navigating the different tax climates and legal climates. Check out http://simplepassivecashflow.com/tax/ for additional information.

Getting from $1 million to $10 million net worth sets apart those creating a legacy, and to create that legacy is to invest alongside people who are like-minded—and know how to keep it fun too!

CHAPTER 4

WHY SYNDICATIONS OVER BRRRR OR TURNKEY RENTALS?

I soon realized there were a lot of really good deals out there with a higher than $2–5 million purchase price. And there was a sweet spot above that and below institutional investors who are getting large deals just to invest the plethora of dumb retirement money (just to appease their retail investors, essentially overpaying for what they're getting, but because they get in such scale, they hide in the $20 to $50 million range). These syndication deals and private placements target the $2 million to $20 million range, roughly to spot out *one in a thousand* deals that achieve higher returns at a good risk/reward profile. I personally focused on workforce-housing apartments because of their recession-proof properties.

When I had eleven rentals in 2015, I knew it wasn't a scalable way of investing. And I found my tribe and other high net worth investors who were already investing in syndications and private placements. A lot of these guys were other high paid doctors, lawyers, engineers, and other working professionals who were ten to twenty years older than me. And I discovered this high-level goal or this high-level vision of being a completely passive investor in dozens of deals, putting no more than 5–10 percent of your net worth into any one of those deals in order to achieve diversification. Note: a classic mom-and-pop investor mistake is to build up to an eight or sixteen units, where they have way more than 10 percent of their net worth in that single asset.

I had a background in rental real estate, and I didn't stray from my original goals of cashflow. I targeted properties that were already cashflowing, but maybe there was some sort of a bad management or under-market rents. Whereas if we just put a little lipstick on the pig and focus in on about $4,000 to $6,000 of rehab per unit (enough to change out the flooring, change out the yellow appliances for black or stainless steel ones, playground equipment on the grounds, and freshen up the look without getting into any big construction activities, like new cabinets or breaking down walls), this is enough to just bump the rent $100 to $150 on already under market rentals.

And a lot of times too with commercial real estate—which is very different from residential, and certainly turnkey investments—the property value is not derived off of comparable sales. It's derived off of the net operating income. If you can go in there and either increase the income, which is primarily our business plan, and/or decrease expenses, you can increase net operating income. And when you divide the increase by the prevailing cap rate for that asset class, in that market, that is the difference in value that you have increased the property. This is not market appreciation, this is called *forced appreciation*. Value comes through those people who create value. And the value that we're creating is better living conditions for tenants who will in turn pay a little bit more rent.

Syndication investing is pulling together passive investor capital so that the operators or your general partners can go after a stronger deal with very low competition (too big for mom-and-pop investors and better deals the clunky institutions can't find). Then implement a business plan once passive investor capital is pooled together.

Securities laws are triggered no differently than creating a company stock; some syndications are done differently, but for the most part, an LLC will own a piece of property and have title to it. That LLC will be split in ownership with all passive investors based on their pro-rata share. All this will be executed through a legal document called the *private placement memorandum* (PPM). If you've never seen a private placement memorandum, you'll probably be very overwhelmed.

It's a pretty hefty document that's over a hundred pages in length with a lot of capital letters yelling at you. We typically pay a lawyer $15,000–$20,000 to put this together and to also do our United States securities filings for us.

A private placement memorandum does two things:

1. It protects the passive investor that the general partners have fiduciary responsibility to not lie, cheat, steal, or run the investment into the ground.
2. It also protects the general partner to help prevent disgruntled passive investors from suing should investment performance not be met.

You could syndicate capital for any type of business or project (real estate or not). I like to invest in real estate assets that are stabilized, which are defined as 90 percent occupied or more so that I can get Fannie Mae or Freddie Mac– agency non-recourse debt, and I can implement a business plan while cashflowing from day one. So, in case anything happens in the economy, like if a recession happens, we'll just continue the cashflow. But if things go well, and even if things go bad, we can still implement the business plan of rehabbing units as vacancies naturally arise because we raised the capital to do all the renovations upfront and because we're property capitalized. And that forced appreciation allows us to possibly even refinance in the interim to strip out equity as tax-free distributions or hold the cash in reserves.

In 2015 I was transitioning to investing in multi-family syndication apartments when I realized that I didn't know too much about the space. It was very different than owning your own rental properties. I knew this was the direction I needed to head, but it really took me eighteen months to really start to put in my first $50,000 on a private placement deal and sign this overwhelmingly large PPM. I paid to be in a group where it got me around other syndication, passive investors and through paid networking events and building relationships with people, I often had to get flights and travel out of state to get there. About eighteen months went by until I had developed a great network of other pure passive investors that I could rely on for good referrals and information.

An internal breaking point came when I had dozens and dozens of people I could rely on, but there were maybe only a few people who were in twentysomething-plus deals. And I had built up the relationship enough to get to a point where I could ask like, *Hey man, so how do these syndications really work? Do you really get the cashflow started and does the pro forma really happen?* And, for the most part, the answer that I got was, out of twenty or so deals, maybe a few of them we lost a little money. We don't know if there was any potential foul play involved. We don't think so, but we don't know for certain. Those are the bad cases.

It wasn't a total loss, *right?* That's why you invest in deals that do non-recourse debt, so that should anything bad happen, barring an embezzlement fraud or anything like that, LPs and GPs are able to just walk away from the debt. So they also said, well, you know, with those few bad ones, maybe we also had a few really good ones that doubled our money in three years. The majority of deals were kind of right where we thought they would be—there should be an 80–100 percent return in five years with little to no effort on their part, other than signing the paperwork in the beginning. The beautiful thing is redeploying your (now doubled) funds into more projects and building up a bigger passive activity losses stockpile in the process.

I made the realization that there's nothing in life that is risk free. But if I, at the age of thirty and just shy of $1 million net worth, could just diversify myself enough, maybe I don't double my money every five years, but if I could grow my money at a 15 percent IRR, I would be on the road to financial freedom, and I would be able to quit my engineering job. So that was when I consciously made the decision that this type of investing was for me. I didn't know anything about the tax benefits back then. I was just kind of going after the highest and best returns for my money that had the best risk adjusted return profile or *Sharpe Ratio*, which is a sort of measurement of risk versus reward.

I just realized I needed to get into a few syndication deals because that was going to help me develop my network even further to find out additional opportunities. As the years go by, you start to realize that these syndication deals are a superior way to invest. They're *stronger* deals. There is much stronger forced appreciation, essentially like a house flip, but with these additional benefits:

1. Income derived off the investment (as opposed to house flips or private money lending) is *passive* income, not ordinary income.

2. You, the LP, if you're going into a *stabilized asset*, you're getting cashflow in the beginning. Normally the cashflow is the smaller part of your returns where the majority of returns come from forced appreciation. Getting cashflow is nice, and in turn, you're sort of de-leveraging your investment right off the bat as the cashflow checks come in; you can also use those cashflow checks just like you would a turnkey rental to either eat off of or to put toward even more investments.

3. Syndicated deals offer better leverage (debt) options with longer loan terms of eight to fifteen years amortized over thirty to thirty-five years.

4. Stronger legal protection as an LP since you're not a managing member of the asset.

5. Better tax benefits due to cost segregations. See https://simplepassivecashflow.com/ costseg/ for more info.
6. Larger institutional asset providing more stability and more economies of scale.

I think the only downside of this type of investing is potentially investing with a shyster. *So, how do you mitigate the risks responsibly?* My solution, was to build my network and to invest with whom those people I trusted (other passive investors) had invested with in the past.

By going through all these mastermind groups, I learned a lot, including many things that LP investors aren't able to do, which is to underwrite the deals themselves by taking the profit and loss statements and rent rolls and putting it into a proprietary model. This allowed me to essentially decode the code, right? I could take the data and figure out if the deal was legitimate or not. When people ask me, "How do you decide what deals to go into?" my general party line is, well, 50 percent of it is vetting the people, which is made possible by making connections with other pure passive Accredited investors.

Some people mistakenly invest off blind social proof, but what also happens sometimes is when operators get a larger following, they start to get a little loose on the underwriting. And also the investor splits start to go down and fees go up. This is what I call "operator creep." So, how not to get fooled by this? The key is working with a good operator or doing the numbers yourself. But again, like I said, this is not within the scope of most passive investor's skill sets. I would say 90–95 percent of LPs don't know how to underwrite the numbers themselves.

First of all, in even the shiniest of pitch decks and webinars, there's nothing in there that tells you the raw data in the first place. It doesn't give you that code to even put into the decoder (model). My personal process is to first underwrite the deal, and the other half of my vetting processes is to spot check these key deal assumptions that ultimately drive the projected return calculations. By determining what kind of assumptions the operator is using, I can see how good the deal is and where the operator is at in the aggressive-conservative spectrum. And if an operator, for example, is assuming rents are going to rise 3 percent every year, or they are using aggressive reversing cap rates that are lower to save 5.5

percent as opposed to 6 percent, I likely will not want to partake in that deal.

Most LPs go around the horn and interview operators (investor relations salespeople), who are trained in telling LPs exactly what they want to hear. And even worse, just find those operators who are better at internet marketing tricks than having a track-record at operating successful real estate projects. I think this is a waste of time. If it were me, I would determine what level of conservativeness the operator runs their numbers on a deal, then go and talk to those who passed that test. I think this is why people like to invest alongside me. Other than our shiny personality (that is partially joke), they do get access to the principal, but more importantly is our level of transparency. I want investors to understand how we run our numbers and therefore understand the margin for the unknown and unknowable that will unfold once a project is underway. Some operators go into a deal where they have to sharpen the underwriting pencil and the "airplane only has half a tank of gas at takeoff." I want investors to understand how much gas we have and for them to make the best investment decision, because once this plane takes off . . . there is no getting off; we're all together for the ride.

A lot of these details on the numbers are outlined in my passive investor syndication e-course for LPs; you're not going to be underwriting specialists, but these are the things that are important to understand as an LP to at least not go into a sucker deal. And once you get yourself up to an intermediate-advanced level through the first few modules, I have a *secret syndication video series,* with the help of my Family Office clients that you should watch. We developed eight sessions where my students go back and forth on different syndication nuances out there. It took me quite a long time to start to write my first check, but education is knowledge, and it will totally allow you to become a better passive investor.

For the free guide, check out
http://simplepassivecashflow.com/syndication/

As I mentioned, a lot of my clients are higher net worth investors who are most likely going to be valuing their time over money. More often than not, part of the issues with being a remote landlord is that you're constantly getting abused by property managers and vendors because they have an assumption about you: you're just some rich person out in California/Hawaii/Seattle who has never seen the property before. Most experienced remote investors get tired of getting gouged on pricing and eventually transition into syndications and private placements with the right people. In 2013–2015 while building my portfolio to eleven remote rentals, I started to run into this problem, and what really bothered me was that I didn't really have any recourse to prevent this. As an engineer in the construction industry, I knew how much things cost. I know how much a couple of dudes' time is worth per their hourly rate. And when I saw a plumbing repair come up as $900, I didn't really get a good explanation from my property manager or plumber . . . I knew what was up!

Something can be said for having a relationship with a property manager, but I didn't really like having a single point of failure and constantly getting price-gouged as an out-of-state investor. Not to mention that direct ownership and management of a rental is not scalable.

We're mostly passive-buy-and-hold investors here. I think house hacking is for kids. Who wants to live next to their tenant? I mean, cool. If you're some bro or a young lady in their twenties, I think that's awesome. This is essentially what I did in my twenties. I worked on the road on the company's dime.

I moved hotel to hotel every week so that I could save $50,000–$100,000 out of my paycheck every single year to plow into buying more rentals. And that's what really helped me accelerate my growth to where I'm at today. But for a lot of people in their forties, fifties, and especially those who are married or have a significant other...the better half may not be willing to I live that way. I think it's a younger person's thing.

There are a lot of tactics like this buy/rehab/ refinance/rent/repeat idea, or BRRRR for short, which I think is another tactic that should only be employed by the lower net worth guys, certainly under a quarter to half a million dollars. The concept sounds pretty sleek: buy a property that needs a lot of work and at a lower price, find a contractor to fix it up (this is the biggest risk in the plan), get a bank to give you a new loan for the higher appreciated value, then rent it out or sell and repeat.

I think the biggest thing is when you're doing this remotely and you're wiring over large sums of money, like $10,000–$50,000, or even more, to acquire a property and put in the capital improvements or the repairs, there's a single point of failure with the people you work with.

Many times, you're working with an unprofessional person. Today, I try not to work with people who have under a couple million dollars net worth or less. They may not value the relationship with me as much as they value putting food on the table for their family by running off with my money or skimping on performance. If a contractor is any good, they eventually swim upstream to work on larger homes that have higher profit margins than slumming it with an out-of-state investor sub-100k property.

I also don't like to really work with people who don't have a college degree. Granted, I don't think college degrees are *that* important these days, but at least this tells me somebody has gone through the process to achieve something that often requires four plus years of focus. Of course, that is just *my* investment criteria, and I believe anyone can choose to be as discriminating as they want when it comes down to investing your own hard-earned money. Don't trust just anyone: be smart, mindful, and follow your gut instincts.

So many people choose to rely on a lot of other people without even vetting any of this stuff. And what is absolutely crazy to me is that so many of the people who do this are *not* in the construction industry to begin with. They don't know how to manage contracts. They don't have any background in this field. For me, I used to do this for a living; we'd always go back and forth about "unforeseen conditions" and discuss managing the scope and budget timelines with contractors. So, a lot of this stuff came as second nature to me. You have smart people (doctors, dentists, accountants and computer programmers, to name a few), of course, but many are definitely out of their realm of expertise in a more blue-collar-type situation of managing construction.

The last issue I have with these BRRRR is that I feel it is a big risk to rely on banks to give you a good refinance via favorable appraisal, which is not necessarily in their best interest. Overall, I think it's a great way to make a lot of money (ordinary, not passive, income in terms of taxes), but I don't think it is a good risk adjusted return to sustainably build wealth over time. Essentially, you're taking more risk than you should be, working with amateur-level talent, rolling the dice on appreciation, not prudent cashflow.

That said, you as the investor need to understand the risk/reward profile and match that with your goals. For most higher net worth clients—myself included—being a passive investor in a larger deal that exhibits cashflow combined with an institutional quality business, which plans to incrementally increase the properties rents over time via forced appreciation, offers more than enough equity growth while supporting the need to hedge the downside risk and preserve your capital in tough economic times.

CHAPTER 5

USING REAL ESTATE TO PAY LESS TAX

Note: I am not a CPA or tax attorney and, therefore, will not be giving any tax advice. But if you're a six-figure earner and are paying more than a 19–29 percent tax rate, pay close attention.

When I was investing in rental properties, I was able to create passive losses through each of my investments. On a basic level, investors are able to take a paper loss on one-twenty-seventh of the price of the improvement value (the value of the building or structure) of the property every year for twenty years.

For example, that first property I owned in Seattle back in 2009 that I purchased for $360,000, I was able to deduct around $7,000 of losses every year in the form of depreciation ($200,000 was the improvement value portion). I was able to use this to lower my ordinary income (since I had an under $100,000 adjusted gross income) or elect to hold on to these losses to offset future gains from the cashflow or eventual sale.

Today, when I buy in places like Alabama, Texas, Georgia, or Florida, the tax benefits are actually stronger, since land values are lower in proportion to the building improvement value. In 2016 when I started to go into syndications and private placements, there was a new tax law that went into effect that allowed for bonus depreciation, which greatly increased the amount of deductions I could extract from the investment as opposed to taking it over twenty-seven years in a straight line depreciation.

With the new favorable laws in place (who knows how long this will last—and eventually be replaced by some other tax best practice), I was able to take one-third of the entire building improvement value all in the first year, giving me a boatload of passive losses, allowing me to build up a surplus to use strategically in the coming years. This aggressive depreciation is totally within the rules of the IRS and is made possible via a cost segregation on the asset. This is basically done on the partnership level within a syndication where they hire a cost segregation expert to go out and itemize all the components of the building. And they hand this big report to the CPA, who then is able to write off the asset more aggressively and give all passive losses accordingly to pro-rata owners, even passive investors (LPs).

As I started to learn from my peers and different mastermind groups, this opened up a myriad of different tax mitigation strategies. By 2017 and 2018, I paid less than a 10 percent effective tax rate. In 2019 I paid zero in taxes.

Depreciation is written into the tax code as a way for business owners or real estate owners to take a paper loss on their assets as the assets slowly decay in terms of serviceable life. A rental property or a commercial asset might last well beyond its twenty- to thirty-year paper depreciation cycle. It may even last a century, but, as far as the tax code goes, there is a serviceable life which you can deduct. This is really what a lot of people don't understand in terms of why real estate is such a great investment class or asset class—there are so many great tax benefits.

I try and keep things simple because, quite frankly, as a passive investor, you don't really need to know the details but know enough to have an informed conversation with your tax professional and to steer them to optimizing the tax code for your benefit—unfortunately, this will make your CPA's job a bit harder and might make them feel uncomfortable if they are not on the cutting edge of the tax code. As a passive investor, I want you to educate yourself just enough to use it effectively in a strategy to get to your end game, which is to effectively pay less taxes. I learned a long time ago that a lot of people out there like to understand every little minute detail these days. Personally, I like to understand things because we discuss these in our Family Office Ohana Mastermind, but for the average passive, high net worth investor out there, there really isn't much sense to learn what goes on in detail, right? Like, when I turn on the TV, I know how to use the remote and turn it on and change the channels. I could even probably record a DVR here and there, but I don't really care about how it all works. When I'm outside, I don't examine the roots on the tree or how the nutrients go up it. But I'll definitely eat and enjoy the fruit; that's for sure.

Most passive, high net worth investors are busy, and most people in my tribe at Simple Passive Cashflow are busy working professionals, oftentimes with a day job and a family life at home. So, let's focus our finite time and energy on our highest and best use, which is likely spending time with our loved ones or at our day jobs, making six figures and above. Let's not get bogged down in the details and focus on what is going to move the needle.

Why the heck do you need passive activity losses and what are they for? Well, there are a couple of major different types of income out there. There is passive income that is derived from our real estate investments and other forms of passive income, and there is ordinary income out there derived from 1099s and W-2 paychecks. Overall, we're trying to move away from ordinary income to passive income because these passive activity losses can offset passive income. So, as we rack up passive activity losses (through depreciation of our real estate), these can be moved forward year to year, and they just become "suspended." When needed, we can use these suspended passive activity losses to offset our passive income that our investments make to pay no taxes.

Many sophisticated investors are walking around with several hundred thousand dollars of passive activity losses suspended in the air, thus able to use it as they realize passive gains to not pay taxes. Now, one strategy that we use for a lot of our clients in our Family Office Ohana

Mastermind is utilizing real estate professional status designation on taxes, or REPS for short.

This is a great strategy where there are some nuances to being able to check this box on your tax return. Assuming you meet the criteria, you're able to use those passive activity losses to offset not only your passive income but your ordinary income from your day job or 1099s. Now, this is extremely valuable for high-paid professionals, such as doctors who might make $600,000 a year, to bring them out of that highest tax bracket; we ideally try and bring them down to around $330,000, thus saving them more than $100,000 like that!

That $330,000 has other significance in other tax planning, because in the year 2021, that is the break between the 24 percent and 32 percent tax bracket. So, as you can see, there's a bit of an art to this. There's no one way of doing it, which is why you need a peer group of other passive investors brainstorming these ideas to then take to your tax professional. But the best I can tell you now is simply to educate yourself and then give you the basic rules of thumb for now; such clients are able to use passive activity losses to strategically pay taxes when they want, and ideally trying to kick the can to the future (utilizing time value of money) or possibly never paying taxes ever.

I'm not a CPA and I'm not a tax professional. But I'm not working a day job anymore. And I figured out how to use the system legally in my favor. And this is how a lot of high net worth, sophisticated investors do it too. The important thing is to arm yourself with the right information so that you can have an educated conversation with your tax professional to steer the ship—after all, these are your taxes. You need to empower yourself and pay attention to this—after all, taxes are your number one expense in life...so pay attention to it!

On the ethics side, a lot of people give high net worth people a lot of crap because they don't pay any taxes. My rebuttal to this is that we're the investors putting our skin on the line, funding investments that are powering this country forward even during times of uncertainty, including pandemics and possible economic slowdowns. The tax code is written to influence behavior and to reward certain behaviors like ours to put allocated funds into these types of places.

For example, the tax code rewards exploratory oil and gas investments because this country needs more self-reliance on domestic oil as opposed to relying on volatile relations in the Middle East. So, the US government offers great incentives to those investing in domestic oil and gas projects. Same can be said for solar or electric vehicles. Now, if you're like most people in America and you just stick your money into the 401(k) retirement mutual funds, you're going to get what everybody else gets and you're going to have to pay taxes. Everybody needs to help the system in certain ways; the way we do things makes Uncle Sam happy and complies with IRS codes; therefore, we don't pay most taxes.

Most CPAs don't know these strategies despite doing a lot of tax returns. Remember, you should only take financial advice from those people who are *financially free*. Numbers don't lie. People's net worth doesn't lie (unless they were a trust fund kid). Many CPAs and financial planners are living paycheck to paycheck; they haven't figured this stuff out yet.

CHAPTER 6

JUST BEFORE I QUIT MY DAY JOB

Back in 2015 I was making a few hundred bucks with my eleven rental properties. I was bringing in a decent cashflow. Of course, this was after all of the property management expenses, repairs, and so on. I really started to see how it was possible to gain financial freedom.

I graduated college in 2007. And I started investing in 2009. So, this is about five or six years down the path of being a real estate investor. I started to realize how little the W-2 paycheck mattered. I had already realized at this point that Santa Claus wasn't real. The Easter Bunny wasn't real, nor was the Tooth Fairy. And I wasn't much of a corporate person.

My engineering job was very stressful, and I was still traveling a lot. I realized I had the option to find a less stressful, less paying job because the real estate more than supplemented my income.

There was one thing that happened for me. And I think this happens for many of my clients. I call it *the pivot point*, the point where something bad happens in their lives. And it's always seemingly bad because, as Tony Robbins says, things happen *for you, not to you.* So, I had an instance in my workplace where I pretty much got thrown under the bus because a project I was in charge of got caught up in a legal- precedence-setting issue. The situation got tough especially with toxic people, and I realized I was just a number in a large company.

Not a day goes by that I'm not thankful I'm no longer working for that employer and that I got sent down a path early. Pretty much everyone who reaches out to me and joins our Investor group has a similar epiphany to some degree. Maybe they get passed up for promotion or they have a boss who's doing shady things and then they get in trouble for it. Or they look at the person they've worked alongside for fifty years and see that all they got for a retirement was— not a watch— a bunch of soggy Chinese fried noodles for their retirement party that nobody really cared to go to. One common thing I see and hear from folks like you is that your peers and boss are typically not there because they are shiny personalities, that are financially free, so they choose to be there on their own accord. No, most people are there for a paycheck, and unfortunately, there might be backstabbing or at least minor office politics to ensure that one "cashflow stream" stays intact.

The one nice thing about having a college education was that I was able to find other jobs. Because I had many rentals at this point, I was able to take less money for a role that was less stressful. I started to work for public government agencies, leaving the high-stress private sector behind. Not only did I find better work environments but better coworkers who weren't cutthroat competitive and actually enjoyed going to work every day. It was nice to go in and interact with people, life just got a lot easier, and that would have been a happily ever after story but . . .

TODAY, I OWN THOUSANDS OF RENTAL PROPERTIES, AND I DO THIS FULL TIME.

As I started to work in more "chill" jobs and have more free time on my hands, I was always thinking about the *next* thing. And I started to realize that my eleven rentals, bringing in a few thousand dollars of passive income every month, was really cool. But out of those eleven properties, I had an eviction or two every year and some big issue or catastrophe every quarter. I've had several instances where evictions lead to big repair bills, up to $20,000.

Single-family homes are a great way to get started. It got my net worth off the ground. Of course, that first $100,000 net worth is always the hardest. But as I started to level-up my network and joined different mastermind groups, I started to realize a lot of these guys invest in private placements and syndications. What was really comforting to know was that a lot of these guys used to do what I did at the time—own single-family homes. And they all said they were so glad to be out of it.

When I started out, I purchased properties in the wrong areas, like Seattle. I eventually moved to more cashflow-based areas in red states with more landlord friendly laws. I got up to a point where I started to transition into syndications and private placements. Keep in mind, this is all within a decade time span. There were definitely mistakes I made along the way, such as paying down debt; sophisticated investors don't do that. Second, investing with the wrong people, which was caused by not having the relationships that would've prevented me from going into bad deals. Plus I paid a heck of a lot of money that should have gone toward investments to learn about all these tax and wealth-building strategies . . . but I am glad I can distill the best practices to you!

THE SYSTEM I'M ADVOCATING FOR IS *NOT* EASY, BUT IT'S VERY SIMPLE. *IT JUST TAKES A WHILE.*

My parents never did any type of real estate investing. They discouraged me from having people rent out my house for fear of bad tenants. I started out with a good job that I parlayed into that first investment. But I thrashed in the water for ten years to get where I am today. Now, I barely use any energy to swim.

Let's take a very typical scenario of somebody who has achieved this "high-speed, low-drag" wealth-building method. They have a large retirement account. They start investing in alternative assets where they know the sponsor personally, so they've cut out the middleman and have gotten better returns backed by hard assets just in case there is a hiccup in the economy. They use their passive losses to offset both their active and passive income. And they start to do all these different tax or wealth-building strategies, such as infinite banking, and they start to realize they can now go to a job because they may love it or even enjoy it, or their spouse can stay at home with their kids because it makes more sense for them to do that. At the end of the day, they net more money because they are paying less taxes. It's a beautiful thing. And they create a lifestyle that is more sustainable for themselves, and they're able to teach the skills to their children, as opposed to enabling them to blow it like 90 percent of wealth lost in the subsequent two to three generations.

I would have been more than happy to keep working as a city engineer with a couple handfuls of rentals. In a great work environment with great coworkers, investing passively in real estate deals and doing all the same tax games to a mid-forties retirement. But I started to create my website (simplepassivecashflow.com), which became very popular, and investors wanted to invest alongside me.

That's when I started the Family Office consulting business to create an opportunity for others to follow the same blueprint I did. And when I made enough revenue from that program, I realized I needed to leave my engineering job because there were people that needed to be lead on the less traveled road to financial freedom.

CHAPTER 7

THE BS IN THE TRADITIONAL FINANCIAL WISDOM

The mission I've been on since leaving my day job is to dispel a lot of the money myths about financial dogma out there. I took the "financial red pill" when I bought my first rental property back in 2009. And I discovered that a lot of the financial tactics of the wealthy are very different than what normal people do. These tactics are very simple but very different than what your mom and dad did, or what they taught you to do. I don't go to a cubicle every day, but I do remember the conversations around the water cooler about putting X amount of money into your 401(k) and average Joe conversations about Bitcoin or Tesla stocks.

You put more money into this 401(k), which relies on the accumulation theory, which says to save up ~$2–4 million while blindly putting your money into this government- or retirement-sponsored plan. And then, when you're old, you can retire. Granted, you won't be as mobile, but you can live off of that big pile of cash. I took a look at this traditional accumulation strategy and realized you need to buy things and that you need cashflow to do that, unless you're going to eat away at your pile of cash.

Stop! Why not begin with the end in mind and create many streams of income today? That's what rental properties or syndications do for you. You're creating multiple streams of income or mini pensions. And the beauty of this is your full-time job will likely pay for your daily living expenses today, but these mini pensions will kick off more cashflows so that you can acquire *more* mini streams of income. By the time you get halfway to critical mass, which is your personal monthly cashflow goal, most people aim for around $10,000 of passive cashflow a month. You get to a point where you can start taking some of that cashflow and really have fun with it now.

A lot of us were good little boys and girls. We went to school, we studied hard, we worked at our jobs and we put our heart, sweat, and tears into it. We invest in everything we're supposed to. Meanwhile, in the shadows, there are these large Wall Street companies. They create retail products for a lot of hardworking Americans to invest in. And what you don't realize is that they're robbing your retirement blind.

This was made so clear to me when I had my first rental property. I was making more than 30 percent return on investment on my money. And I looked over at my 401(k) at 8 to 10 percent. And then I was like, *Where did all my money go? What's happening here?*

I started to invest in real estate and was getting higher returns and realized that Wall Street was a system to extract maximum profits via hidden fees for them! I was doing a lot of index funds when I was starting out. Of course, I'm not advocating for people to leave their day jobs and spend a whole bunch of time on their investments. Just do enough to get the minimum effective dose. See what happens to your net worth when your money grows at 15–20 percent a year compared to the more conventional 8–10 percent per year.

Look at where you end up five, ten, fifteen years in the future. You can download the Net-Worth Tracker Sheet at http://simplepassivecashflow. com/legacy/

If you follow what the herds do, you're going to get slaughtered with them. If everybody did what I did and bought a few prudent cashflow rentals, and eventually paid them off in the future, who would work? Who would get our coffees. Who would design bridges? Who would do root canals for us? You might do it because you enjoy the work and you like to help people, but in the grand scheme of things, society might crumble.

One of the biggest financial mistakes I see people making is blindly buying the house they live in. The house you live in does not make you much money other than the mere fact of keeping up with the pace of inflation. Whereas when you're buying assets, such as rental properties or syndications, you're making money *four* ways: the appreciation is on par with buying your house, but you're also getting money with cashflow, tax benefits, and the fact that your tenant is paying down your mortgage (this is the big difference, where another family is putting in their heart, sweat, and tears to pay down your mortgage for you so that you can accumulate equity), and then the appreciation.

I know younger families want to live near their jobs, but most times they can't afford it. They want a large house for their kids to run around the yard and play in, and they want to be in a good school district. So, what do they do? They buy that house—that *expensive* house—and now they lose that large down payment that should have gone into deals and they are saddled with a huge mortgage that jacks up their monthly cashflow.

If you're looking at a $600,000 house, which is a starter home for most, you're talking about nearly $150,000 of capital that you need to save. If you could do it, you're probably in the top tier of Americans who can actually save that much, so, congratulations, and by the way, you have definitely found your tribe or frugal savers at http://simplepassivecashflow.com! But what you could have done with that money is purchase five turnkey rentals or a handful of completely passive syndication deals that each make you a few hundred dollars of cashflow every single month. So, you'd have five sets of tenants paying your mortgage every single month. Something you're not going to have when you buy your house since you're the only one paying down your mortgage. You're going to be doing all the work to do that. Whereas when you buy rental properties or get into syndication deals, people are paying down this debt for you. Think of it as leveraging your own personal self, the tax benefits, times five rental properties.

Of course, when you're in syndication deals, you get the forced appreciation potential of turning units and bumping rents. When you buy this big house, the supposed American Dream, you're just burdened with this big mortgage and, for most, a $3,000 monthly mortgage is huge.

From a high level, that large mortgage is taking away your cashflow. Now, cashflow is a very important thing. And, in this respect, I see it as oxygen, the lifeline of your finances. Now, a lot of these folks have some emotional attachment to the house. I get it. Maybe you like the idea of buying rental properties and building up your asset column to increase your cashflow, but now you take a gut punch to your monthly cashflow and future ability to save future down payments on future acquisitions.

A big caveat here is that most people *should* buy a house. I'm talking about the people who aren't great at saving or managing money because a house is a forced savings account. And most people are really horrible with their money. If they have $500 laying around, they spend it. Most people have credit card debt. Most people don't put away 10–20 percent of their paycheck to savings or investments.

But you're different.

You're one of the diligent folks who are financially free. So, this is a double-edged sword. If you do this the wrong way, it can hurt you. But if you're good with your money, you can take that free capital to buy assets: rental properties, syndication opportunities, and the like, and you can grow your net worth much more quickly, and more prudently and safely in one of the most proven hard asset classes out there.

A lot of my clients are investing in a 529 college savings plan for their kids, a 401(k) for themselves, or other government retirement vehicles when they first come to me. The big problem I have with this is, you're confined to retail investments which are for the masses. And they are laden with hidden fees, right?

IF YOU DO WHAT EVERYBODY ELSE IS DOING, YOU'RE GOING TO GET WHAT EVERYBODY ELSE GETS.

The available investments in these kinds of programs are just like the crappy cafeteria options in high school. But I'm giving you that magical "off-campus pass" that gives you the opportunity to go off in your car and eat wherever you want. There needs to be a little bit of due diligence around it, of course, but you open up a wide blue ocean of better investment options.

My recommendation is not to do any 529 plans; instead, do an infinite banking policy, which utilizes life insurance in a very unique way. And a REIT (Real Estate Investment Trust) is just a bastardized mutual fund of real estate holdings, which we're trying to get away from. It's kind of like going shopping at Neiman Marcus or Nordstrom. You're getting the same thing but you're just paying way too much. Most of my clients and other Simple Passive Cashflow–Nation members prefer to buy the basic stuff at nonretail pricing. So REITs are like the retail version of investing. What I'm advocating for is to take a little bit of ownership in your portfolio. It doesn't take too much education. It will require building up a bit of a peer network of pure passive investors who can help you to choose between good deals and bad ones. However, this will allow you to get better returns while investing in more recession proof assets.

Another principle we follow is investing in deals where we know the operator directly, and we cut out all the middlemen. Crowdfunding websites operate as electronic middlemen; they're making money and charge the real estate operator heavy fees to list their deal, which ultimately comes out of the investors cut. This is why my investment firm does not use crowdfunding websites to raise capital for us because (1) we have a loyal investor base and (2) I don't want to pay their exorbitant fees. When I invest in syndication deals and private placements as an LP, I want to know the operator personally. Second, I want to cut out all these unnecessary marketers and middlemen who ultimately take my returns out of my pocket.

Normal, conventional financial advice tells us life insurance is sort of a scam, *right?* But remember the financial gurus you see on TV, they're catering toward the financially irresponsible and immature. They're telling people not to go into debt to the people who are unable to determine the difference between good and bad debt.

What the wealthy do is they bank on themselves. They use one of the most secure investment vehicles out there, which is life insurance contracts with AAA-rated insurance companies, which have been around for centuries. They're backed by insurance companies, which invest for long-term capital preservation. These are the guys who own the large skyscrapers and the class-A assets.

With life insurance and infinite banking, the underlying trick is that it's using whole life insurance, a product that a lot of us are aware of but may have a stigma attached to it. The way it's customized and configured turns it into what we're trying to use it for, which is a store of capital. There are three major ways to configure these policies, and when you increase one, there is a tradeoff and takes away from the other. What we're trying to do here is to *increase the amount of liquidity* that we have; liquidity is us putting money into the policy but being able to take a loan from the policy the next day, therefore taking that money and investing it in assets that produce more income for us, like rentals or syndications.

We try to maximize this leverage, but to do that we need to customize the policy to minimize the amount of returns we get and minimize the amount of death payout—which most insurance providers will probably think you're crazy for doing. Why would you not use the whole life product to increase returns? Well, this is what a lot of high net worth families do. And these are the secrets of the wealthy, so pay attention because here is the trick.

What we're trying to do is give up the death-payout component and the returns or interest rate that the policy generates in order to maximize liquidity because that liquidity is going to arm us with capital to invest in much higher yielding investments, allowing us to grow our net worth faster. All this in an account that grows tax-free because of some IRS tax code that deems it tax-free. Plus, another perk is that your life-insurance account is essentially free from litigators.

Now we're going to beat up on 401(k) plans and retirement accounts, including Roth IRAs. As stated earlier, we don't like 401(k) plans and other employee-sponsored plans because they trap us in a cafeteria of crappy investment options that are very profitable for the investment broker. But in some cases, you're able to self-direct these accounts and get out of the garbage cafeteria and into alternative assets, such as real estate.

Of course, you'll hear people who say, *What do you mean you don't have a retirement account? What will you retire off of?* Little do they know I have several thousand rental properties; these are my retirement accounts. It just doesn't happen to be in a government-qualified retirement plan. If you're one of those people who can't keep your hands off of your money, or segregate your retirement funds from your "spend this month" money or "spend this year" pile, cover your eyes right now. But I think most people reading are able to segregate their piles of money. I think the biggest reason why people say to do retirement plans is because it grows tax-free, which is true, but we're going to break down several reason why not to use such an account; there are more cons to do so.

This is the first reason why we don't use retirement accounts: look at where the tax brackets are today. Most financial wisdom is predicated on an assumption that you're going to get old and stop working in your job and that your adjusted gross income will go way down. But most reading this book, myself included, are going to make a lot *more* money in the future because we're growing our net worth with prudent investments that are spewing off cashflow, which gets to a point where you hit your critical mass and you grow your money faster than you can spend it.

You're likely to be making more money in the future. Therefore, you're going to be in a higher tax bracket. So, pay your taxes today (while in a lower tax bracket), instead of in the future.

Point number two: the government just pumps free, made up money into the system. *How are they going to pay for all these government entitlement programs?* (Side note: on one hand, they're going to increase inflation, which is an insidious way of diluting away their debt—so, to mitigate this, you want to hold hard, tangible assets, such as real estate, which is basically a hedge against inflation. This is the case of why certain debt is good.)

But back to how the government will pay for all this money other than increasing taxes in the future.

Just call me a bit of a Negative Nancy, but I don't see taxes coming down in the future. So pay your taxes now while the tax percentages are lower.

Don't pay taxes on this pile in the future when they'll likely be higher.

When your money is in a retirement plan, you're not getting taxed on it while it's in there. You're making a deal with Uncle Sam where they get to tax you at whatever rate in the future. The untaxed money currently stored away in people's retirement plans is the greatest potential source for government revenue. You bet they know it's there, which is another reason why potentially all the financial dogma is to put money in the 401(k).

Point number three: a lot of us who invest and grow our money at non-retail investment rates are likely to be financially free in under a decade. Most of my investors are able to save at least $30,000 and some of the better ones are able to save up to $100,000 a year. So, the retirement age for a lot of these people is today! I just like the option to get at this pile of money to do whatever I want with it, whenever I want. We're cracking the paradigm on financial literacy and conventional financial wisdom here.

Lastly, here is the game changer for syndication investors: take advantage of the current tax laws of bonus depreciation via cost segregations. By going into larger deals, you're able to get a whole bunch of passive losses that you can potentially use to offset your taxes. The wealthy like to use these passive losses to potentially lower their tax rates today, or whenever they have a higher income year. So, there's a bit of an art form to this, but it's a lever that—when you have these passive activity losses—you're able to control how much taxes you'd pay. When you're investing in a retirement plan, you don't have the ability to use these tax benefits that come from your investments. So, a lot of investors will invest via a self-directed IRA, a solo 401(k), but they don't get the passive losses from their investments. Plus they are also subject to a UDFI tax and other taxes on the leverage portion of their investment, which gets a little tricky. In the grand scheme of things, it's simply better not to invest through any of these qualified retirement plans, which are 401(k)s, IRAs, Roth IRAs, and the like.

As I started to invest and acquire multiple properties and then go into syndications, private placements, and joining different masterminds, I noticed a lot of these money myths were something that folks laughed about. And they're laughing at themselves because they were duped into thinking these were all true: buy a house to live in, invest in retirement plans, work at your job for fifty years, and so on. I went through a phase where all I was trying to do was gain financial independence and get to a point where I didn't have to do anything. And I think a lot of us have that type of mindset: we want to get to a point where we are financially free so that we can travel and do what we want, with whom we want, when we want.

I was very fortunate to get into this mindset pretty early and these ideas started to percolate in my head like, *What would my life look like after I had more than $20,000 of passive cashflow a month?* And something that kept resonating with me were these financial money myths out there, hurting a lot of hardworking, high-quality people and the shrinking middle class that pays more than their fair share of taxes. Because it sure isn't the wealthy doing it and it sure isn't the lower class doing it.

These are the people powering society with their contributions through their work and professions. I just thought it was really sad and unfortunate for a lot of hardworking folks, so I set off on this mission to help out those hardworking professionals duped into these financial myths.

CHAPTER 8

CONCLUSION

When you're a passive investor, the most important thing is to network with other passive investors. When you're in the first half of financial building life (under $250,000–$500,000 net worth), buying single-family home rental properties, you're going to need referrals to find out which brokers to work with, who to work with as a lender, and most importantly, who to have as a property manager. You definitely don't want to go to Yelp or any other review site.

YOUR NETWORK IS YOUR NET WORTH.

This is so much truer when your net worth goes over $500,000 and you're developing into a passive Accredited investor. *Why do you want to work off referrals? And why do you want to build your network?* Syndications, private placements, turnkey rentals, and the like are way better than traditional retail investments, but the one thing that can go wrong is working with the wrong people. How do you mitigate that risk? And how do you verify that? It's crucial to have a network of other passive investors that you have organic relationships with to help point you in the right direction. And eventually, you can help and give back to your own community.

You're investing in syndications and private placements and starting to implement the strategies of the wealthy as you start to meet other passive-investor peers and swap best practices. At this point, you throw anything you hear from your parents and your coworkers about money out the window.

People in my Family Office Ohana Mastermind rejoice because they're finally around their tribe of hardworking professionals interested in growing their wealth.

The first syndication I went into was in 2013, where I found a group to invest with through a referral from a self-directed IRA firm. It was better than nothing, right? It's not like I went to Google or Yelp. That's probably one of the worst ways to go because all you're doing is finding the yo-yos out there who are good at internet marketing.

The lesson learned was that that referral wasn't the gold standard of referrals because the person making the referral himself was a random person! And, because of that, I got unlucky and invested with the wrong person and effectively lost all my money. The golden rule is only work with people who somebody in your organic network can verify, attest to investing with, and has had a positive experience.

My students come to me these days and they'll show me a deal, and the first thing I always ask is, *Who do you know that has actually invested with this person in the past?* And they'll say, "Well, I just saw this on the internet or somebody randomly sent me this email. I don't know how they got my email address." Again, the gold standard is going off referrals off people you trust.

But initially, I didn't have that, and you're not going to have this network from the start. You're going to have to put one foot in front of the other and take small test investments to build a track record of a non-tire kicker (newbie investor) so that you can, in turn, build your peer network up. Just because you're another rich Accredited investor doesn't mean you add value to other rich Accredited investors. Sometimes the best way to add value is unfortunately going into a bad deal, like how I did, and telling others to stay away from that individual. Remember, the long-term goal is to build these organic relationships with other pure passive investors. If you owned a rental or two before and have some war stories to display some experience, that helps too.

The goal here is to find other high net worth Accredited investors who are also investing in these types of private placements, syndications, and the like. The advice you hear a lot out there is to go to the local real estate club, Meetup, or hit up some free forums. In my opinion, this is a complete time-waster because you're finding a lot of people who are broke.

I didn't have very much money at one time. But a lot of what people hear about real estate is house flipping, wholesaling houses, or the general get-rich-quick thing. And you're just not going to meet the right pedigree in these free groups, in person or online. You're trying to find other high net worth Accredited investors who are also doing the same thing that you want to do: be passive and not hang out with a bunch of broke guys at a real estate happy hour. And to compound the problem, Accredited pure passive investors value their privacy too and don't want to flaunt their wealth.

For example, a strategy you see on the internet forums is a bunch of kids doing the BRRRR (Broke people) strategy: buy, rent, rehab, refinance, and repeat, or BRRRR. It works, but it's just not scalable. It's just not a strategy that those who have good paying jobs, making six figures and above should do for various reasons. It takes a lot of time and you have to rely on lower net worth vendors.

I've been able to use my podcast's popularity to attract investors to our virtual and in person community events. And I also keep things pretty confidential; we run our organization to protect people's identities and operate with a certain level of discretion. Of course, I made the *simple passive cashflow podcast*, which became a lightning rod to attract other passive investors. If you're reading this book and haven't booked a free on-boarding coaching call, please check out my website and sign up as soon as possible, as I typically have a few of these calls a day and I don't know how much longer I can keep doing them.

We talked a lot about turnkey rentals, but they may not be your jam either. If you're an Accredited investor, you may go straight into syndications and private placements. Just be cognizant of where you are and what you should be doing; hopefully on our quick call I can remove as much noise and give you a clear path forward based on your personal situation.

How do you get started here? We're talking about building your network with the right people. Granted, you're not going to have that solid group for quite some time, possibly a year or a few years, based on the 70/20/10 principle, where 70 percent of people are actually going out there and doing it, putting some skin in the game. Twenty percent of your education will come from other people, but you should first learn as much as you can academically, which is the 10 percent of effective learning. I normally recommend that new people take at least 3-6 months and learn everything as if you're a sponge.

Learn a little bit about wholesaling properties, flipping properties, and so on. But quickly come off of that and start to narrow in on what *you* should be doing if you're a passive higher net worth investor. The second big thing to do is to build at least one or two people in your corner who you trust to help you. Just double check before you actually put some money into a deal or in an investment. I have a lot of onboarding calls with new investors and sometimes I'm like, *Seriously, where did you get that idea?*

They may have read a book or two, but it's totally out of touch with reality; having at least one or two people in your corner really helps calibrate you to what you're learning. Again, this is highly advised but many people will not have this when they begin.

Genuinely educate yourself on the right passive investing content. I offer a lot of free guides on my website. It's my mission to put information out there for the masses and for whoever is willing enough to put in the effort to learn it. But if you want a more curated experience that is going to save you a lot of time, check out the syndication e-course for LPs or for the remote investor turnkey e-course.

I had three large pivot points in my investing journey. First was renting out my home and becoming a landlord. I accidentally put myself in the right position and then I consciously bought my next property in Seattle. I got a tenant in there and then I moved and focused on a goal and went and achieved that. Then, in 2012, I realized I wasn't cashflowing in Seattle due to the low rent-to-value ratios. So, I went out-of-state investing a couple of thousand miles away in Birmingham, Alabama—in a property I didn't even visit. I did a test investment. I bought one property and it worked. So, in the next few years, I had eleven of those turnkey rentals. I tried out the remote investor thing. I got proof of concept. Then I was all in. In 2015, as I saw that turnkey rentals weren't entirely scalable, I went into my first syndication deal and wrote that $50,000 check and signed a hundred page document that made no sense to me.

I just learned more and more. I had built relationships with many, many investors who gave me the confidence that I was doing something real. Once I got some returns, I eventually sold off all my single-family-home rentals without doing a 1031 exchange, paying no taxes because of built-up passive losses, and went all in to being a syndication investor. My progression probably took a lot longer than yours because you have the framework that I didn't have; I was walking around in the dark—alone.

My approach was to try it out, do a test investment, get proof of concept, then move more heavily into it. But too often, people don't do anything. If you keep doing what everybody else is doing, if you're going to keep investing through your 401(k) or all the options in the crap cafeteria, we know what's going to happen. If you're okay with that known outcome, then I'm happy for you. You're satisfied? Cool. But there's a prudent way to go about doing this that gets you so much more, so much faster and safer. And, in my opinion, investing in more stable investments where capital preservation is key, the hardest part is just getting started. So, take action.

EVERYTHING I'VE OUTLINED TO THIS POINT, FROM BUILDING YOUR NETWORK TO EDUCATING YOURSELF, I DID IT ALL BY MYSELF.

I didn't have a mentor helping me along the way. Maybe I was a little bit more resourceful than the average bear out there, but it took a lot of time. I mean, it took me from 2009 to get to this point today. In 2015, that's the big milestone when I had eleven single-family-home rentals and made the move to syndications and private placements as an Accredited investor. Time is money and money is time, but for a lot of us, time is more valuable than money.

For a lot of us, time is more important. If you want access to my personal rolodex of pure passive and Accredited investors, lenders, brokers, property managers, lawyers, accountants, CPAs, and other vendors, you're going to need to opt into the paid offerings I have. If you're a younger, newer investor looking to pick up your first rental property, I offer a spinoff group called The Incubator, which helps you purchase your first rental property.

I've created a vision in my business where I want to work with high-quality people and create a community of those who want to hit financial freedom and give back. At the end of the day, I enjoy talking and writing about finances. This stuff changes a lot all the time, and it's definitely a hobby of mine.

Going into good deals is just one part of the whole flow chart. Going into good deals that do cost segregations to extract out a lot of bonus depreciation and passive losses allow us to implement many tax strategies to lower our taxable burden, which we've covered in great detail. But this allows us to keep more in our pocket and to then invest more, which creates a harmonious cycle. It's a good, happy, infinite loop to grow our net worth faster. And then we start to employ different higher net worth strategies, such as infinite banking via whole life insurance and start investing from there out of that vehicle, while overlaying other legal strategies that the wealthy do.

This is exactly why the rich get richer and those doing what everybody else is doing stay where they're at. Once you get to a point where you hit a certain critical mass number, which is your passive cashflow number—where you don't have to work anymore—but when your mind learns about these strategies and starts to slowly implement them, you hit a point of zero gravity which some people also refer to as escape velocity. Imagine you're on a rocket taking off from earth. There's so much effort to get one inch off the ground. Some people will say it takes half of the fuel just for that initial lift.

To get that first $100,000 is the hardest part. But then the work doesn't stop there, right? You've got to take this rocket from a foot off the ground to get it out of the atmosphere. And that is getting to this point of your passive cashflow number. For some frugal people, all they need is $5,000 passive a month to hit that escape velocity and break out of the Earth's atmosphere. For most, that number is probably double or triple.

But this is not a get rich quick thing.

It is certainly a get rich *surely* strategy and to grow your net worth from there. I'm confident you can do it; take control of your financial future *today*.

We can help you do that. Join our community at http://simplepassivecashflow.com/club/

About the Author

After twelve years as a Licensed Professional (PE) Civil/Industrial Engineer, Lane Kawaoka fired the boss and began to focus 100 percent of his time on investing and helping others through his Family Office Ohana Mastermind.

He began investing in 2009 in rainy Seattle, and being a ramen-eating cheapo, he was able to buy a property early on right after college. After discovering the difference between *cashflow investing* and *appreciation investing* (gambling/ speculating), he moved his portfolio into eleven single-family rentals in Birmingham, Atlanta, Indianapolis, and Pennsylvania.

Today, Lane operates syndications so that other investors can join in on the benefits of investing in class C & B multi-family apartments, RV parks, mobile homes, and assisted living facilities, because of this nation's demand for affordable housing—not rich people class-A assets. His mission is to help regular people get into good deals that were once only accessible to the rich. And to teach those with an open mind the simple tactics of the wealthy.

The passive income from investing in stabilized rental properties made it possible for Lane to move back home to Hawaii, where the cost of paradise is 10 percent, or more, the cost of living and 30 percent less pay for comparable jobs in the US mainland. There, he was able to live a lifestyle where he was able to bike to work. It did not take him long, however, to finally quit the day job and ditch the e-bike for a Mercedes, Cadillac, Ford Raptor, or whatever childish toy he wished to buy and fund with pure passive cashflow from his investments.

Lane still rents his primary residence in Hawaii because he still thinks buying a home to live in is a waste of money. He thinks if he can be a good example for a young person to not make the most debilitating financial mistake of their life of buying their home before their net worth hits $1 million or more, then the self-sacrifice would be worth it.

Annoyed by the bogus real estate education programs out there (that take money from people who don't have it in the first place), Lane set out to make this free website (simplepassivecashflow. com) to help other hardworking professionals and the shrinking middle class dispel the Wall Street dogma. Simple Passive Cashflow eschews traditional wealth-building methods and offers an alternative to "garbage" investments in the 401(k)/mutual funds that only make the insiders rich.

Today, Lane works to help the hardworking middle class build real asset portfolios by providing free investing education, podcasts, and networking, plus access to investment opportunities not offered to the general public.

Made in the USA
Las Vegas, NV
03 January 2023

64847910R00080